Project Management:

A Practical Beginners Guide to Becoming a Master Project Manager with Any Project

Table of Contents

Introduction

Congratulations on downloading *Project Management: A Practical Beginners Guide to Becoming a Master Project Manager with Any Project* and thank you for doing so. Regardless of what industry you work in, project management is a skill that is always in high demand. A great project manager is worth their weight in gold for the skills they bring to the table and the effortless way that they manage to bring a large and disparate group of individuals together and unite them around a common goal. As the job market becomes even more specialized, business owners know that when they absolutely, positively need a project to be completed successfully, then bringing in a good project manager is the only way to go.

Unfortunately, learning the skills require to manage projects effectively is easier said than done which is why the following chapters will discuss everything you need to get started down the path to managing projects successfully, begining with all the details about just what managing a project entails. You will also learn every attribute you need to possess in order to manage projects effectively as well as how to cultivate them for yourself.

Furthermore, you will learn what it takes to plan a project successfully while communicating with the team at full force and still keeping stakeholders as happy as can reasonably be expected. Finally, and perhaps most importantly, you will learn what it takes to power through the worst when it happens to ensure your project is always completed on time no matter what.

There are plenty of books on this subject on the market, thanks again for choosing this one! Every effort was made to ensure it is full of as much useful information as possible, please enjoy!

Chapter 1: Understanding Project Management

There is a lot of talk these days about project management and its many different applications across different fields, and while much of this talk is centered around getting the  most out of the practice, there is little space given to the discussion of what sets it apart from the regular managerial practices someone in that position might otherwise undertake. To that end, before you can become the best project manager possible, it is helpful to have a clear understanding of just what doing so actually entails.

At its core, project management is about facilitating a specific task that was undertaken with a specific goal, and its related benefits (the project), in mind at its inception. As such, it encompasses the tasks related to planning out what is going to be done and then ensuring that the required steps are taken to ensure the desired results come to fruition as quickly and effectively as possible. Thus, the biggest difference between project management and traditional management is that project management has a specific goal and timeframe for completing that goal from the start.

While small companies may find it unnecessary to implement a formal approach to project management, you will often find that it is essential for everything outside of the simplest projects. While it may not seem like it at first, with practice, you will find that the extra control that a formal approach to managing projects provides will help you to more easily manage complicated task that involve larger groups of people or teams that are spread out through multiple departments or even across the world when they are working remotely. Even the most routine projects are subject to some amount of change during their lifetime, and effective project management can help you to accurately determine the amount of risk that is involved with this as well.

The concept of the project is not unique to any one sector or industry and can be seen everywhere from corporate America to construction, to product manufacture, IT, transportation and more. Despite the wide variety of variation between all these various industries they can all use the same general steps and techniques when it comes to planning out the phases of their projects and ensuring they are followed through to completion successfully.

Project management processes
There are a wide variety of different management processes that are commonly used as a sort of shorthand to ensure that project managers can quickly and easily do everything from calculating risk,

to making schedules, to estimating budgets, to controlling or planning tasks. Each of the major processes related to project management are outlined below.

Monitoring: The first part of any project is the planning stage where the specific details related to the timeframe and cost of various parts of the project are outlined in exhaustive detail. The process of monitoring can then be thought of as keeping track of all of these details and then ensuring that they match up with the reality of the situation both in terms of the amount of time required as well as any related costs. Regularly monitoring the situation makes it much easier to update things like milestones, deadlines and estimates as needed without having to do a lot of extra work in order to do so.

Control: A good product manager needs to control the progress of the project in question without resorting to micromanaging to get things done. The project manager is supposed to facilitate the success of the team, not direct every action that every member makes. This means that the best project managers step in when problems arise to control their spread and understand any related risks to the project and ensure they are as well mitigated as possible before getting out of the way of the team so they can proceed as anticipated.

Communication: The project manager is always going to be ensuring that there is a steady flow of communication between various entities related to the project. This could be between team members in different areas, between the team and higher ups or with anyone else the team needs to be in contact with. This type of process can be both official and unofficial as the project manager will need to keep an ear to the ground and suss out what the feelings of the team are, not just the surface level communication.

Managing People: A good project manager understands the strengths and weaknesses of every member of their team and works to ensure that the strengths of the whole work to cancel out individual weaknesses. Happy team members are effective team members which means that it is as much the project manager's job to ensure that there are no emotional barriers in the way of the project in addition to ensuring all physical, financial and practical barriers are cleared as well. It is not all about motivation, unfortunately, as the project manager is also going to want to be in charge of delivering constructive feedback and cracking the whip to ensure things proceed at the expected pace.

Project Management Phases
In addition to having several common go to processes, project managers are going to see the same project management phases in practically every project. The

details of each project management phase are outlined below.

Initiation: The earliest phase of any project is the initiation phase which is used to determine the case for the project in question which includes what the hopeful gain of the project is as well as any other justifications for its existence. It will also include things like the scope of the project in question as well as an outline of the steps that will be taken to achieve it. This is also the point during the project that every major player is going to be assigned their specifics tasks. This phase is crucial to every successfully managed project as it is the baseline that the project manager will use to gauge success and overall progress towards the project's completion.

Planning: With an overall goal in mind, the planning phase will include filling in all of the specifics related to the project and how it will successfully be completed. From a project management stance this will also include things like the expected timetable, the expected costs, details regarding communication and notes on how the project will be monitored as well as controlled when necessary. The planning document is the one which is likely going to be referred to the most throughout the project completion process which means it is important that it includes a breakdown of the schedule for every relevant task that completing the project is ultimately going to require.

From there, the list should will need to be order in such a way that there is an obvious through line when it comes to successfully completing the project as a whole. This list will need to be as detailed as possible so that every member of the project team will never have a question about what they should currently be doing and what part of the project they will undertake next. The details related to project planning can be found in chapter 3.

Requirements: The requirements for a given project are going to likely be iterated upon through the project's road to completion as the requirements for success are likely going to change multiple times from start to finish. The written list of requirements will need to include the current specific aim of the project along with any relevant constraints on its success as well as the currently expected date of completion. This is the documentation that those outside the project will be able to use to get a generalized overview of the current level of progress.

Execution: Once every member of the team is clear on how the project is going to proceed as well as all of the relevant information required to ensure that their part of the project is completed successfully, all that is left to do is let the team execute on the project successfully. The project manager will want to monitor the progress on the project while at the same time ensuring that all members of the team are on the same page when it comes to determining when a given task has been completed successfully. The project manager will also need to ensure that everyone knows when any relevant details or time frames have changed when compared with the original project outline.

Closure: After a project has been completed, the final phase is always the closure phase which occurs when the project manager can sit down with all of the information related to a particular project, including pre-project estimates as well as an outline of related actual numbers to compare them too. The goal in this phase is to determine not only if the project was an overall success or failure but if it successfully met expectations as well. This phase is crucial to improving the overall process of the team in the long term and should never be overlooked even when the project in question will not be repeated.

Chapter 2: Attributes of a Successful Project Manager

When it comes to determining what sets the best project managers apart from the rest, the answer is easy. Those at the top of their game are always able to finish their projects on time and under budget while at the same time exceeding expectations of the higher ups. They manage to do so successfully time and again because they all exhibit the following attributes and while certain predilections will make some of the following attributes more difficult to hone in yourself than others, with enough practice you can successfully exhibit each and every one of them yourself.

The ability to plan ahead: The best project managers seem to have the ability of precognition, cutting off potential problems at the pass and ensuring things are back to running smoothly before anyone else is even really aware that there is a problem. They don't actually possess the gift of second sight, however, they are just able to anticipate what problems are likely to occur based on past experience and a logical outlook on the state of the project as a whole. The easiest way to improve your own ability to plan ahead is to gain experience in your chosen industry to the point where you have a good grasp on everything that can be seen and done.

Other than waiting years for your experience to accrue, the best way to get better at planning for potential worse case scenarios is to simply sit down and devote the time and energy to brainstorming everything that has the possibility to derail your current project and then sketch out rough ideas of how you would go about staying on course if any of those events come to pass. If you feel as though you aren't taking enough possibilities into account, you may find it helpful to look into any details on past projects that failed as well as the reasons why. Remember, forewarned is forearmed.

The ability to remain organized: A good project manager is organized, not just when things are running smoothly but even during moments that are utterly chaotic. This, in turn, allows them to always remain focused on the big picture and to determine the best course of action in the moment without lots of deliberation or back and forth clogging up the works. While some people are naturally more organized than others, this is another attribute that is primarily going to improve with practice. Only by experiencing plenty of similar situations in the past will you be able to keep your head while everyone around you is losing theirs.

To increase this attribute as quickly as possible you are going to want to start by organizing your workspace as effectively as possible to ensure that you will need to spend as little time as possible actively searching for key items. Organization often occurs as part of a domino effect which means that after you take the time to organize your space you will spend less time looking for things which means you will then be able to take the extra time to ensure all the project documentation is organized efficiently and the effect snowballs from there.

If you just can't seem to organize your personal space, you might be pushing against a mental block that can't be moved via traditional means. If you have issues with organization, stop looking at it as such and instead consider always putting documents or other things related to the project at hand in the same place one day at a time. With enough repetition, a habit will naturally start to develop and you will find that you are becoming more organized despite yourself. When you find that you are able to keep a certain portion of your space organized regularly, don't rest on your laurels, repeat the process with another unorganized area and wait for the positive results to speak for themselves.

The ability to lead indirectly: The project manager of a project team is often not the direct superior to one or more members of the project team which means that they cannot result to many of the more common leadership techniques that managers can resort to when needed. Nevertheless, they are still going to be required to motivate individuals who may or may not always be completely in line with the goals of the project. At the same time, the project manager is going to need to be able to stand up to outside sources who might have influence on the project and protect the team from outside interference as needed.

While every project manager is going to lead differently, your end goal should be to utilize your natural talents to enhance the type of leadership that you ultimately embody. It is important to avoid being too hands on or aggressive, however, as this will only result in you making members of the team less willing to make concessions to you in the future, a death knell for an effective project manager. Rather, you will want to get to know each member of the team personally in an effort to understand what types of stimuli they respond best to. While it might seem manipulative, learning to push team members' buttons effectively is a key part of ensuring the project proceeds smoothly.

The ability to communicate effectively: When it comes to communication, a project manager is always going to have numerous different pots in the fire simply because different sections of constituents are going to require different information. First and foremost, the project manager is going to want to facilitate conversation between different subgroups of the project team to ensure that they spend their time working towards successfully completing the project and not worrying about getting in touch with one another for various bits of relevant information.

Additionally, the project manager is going to need to discuss details with outside concerned parties in such a way that is accurate while still allowing the team as much freedom to complete the project in question as possible. Finally, the project manager may be called upon to discuss the project in a more forward facing way with the target audience of the business in question.

This attribute requires the ability to compartmentalize information and keep separate streams of information in mind to ensure that relevant information gets where it needs to be while at the same time not getting scrambled from the source message. Censoring out relevant information is key to being a successful project manager as it can be easy to flood various different types of individuals with a torrent of essentially useless information that will, at best, make it more difficult to parse other more relevant information that you provide them with; or at worst, impede the progress of the project as they try and make an irrelevant piece of information into a big issue because they do not understand the full context. Information is a powerful thing and the best project managers treat it as such and only dole it out in relevant chunks.

The ability to focus on the end goal: The best project managers are all about getting the project finished first and foremost. This certainly means that they plan out the best course of action and then monitor it to ensure things proceed as anticipated, but it also means that they understand that sometimes the plan is simply going to have to change on the fly and then act accordingly. This, in turn, is not a rash reaction, but instead a measured approach to the changing marketplace that takes into account all relevant variables to ensure that the overall course of action is still the one that will the see the project successfully completed on time and under budget.

The easiest way to improve your ability to act pragmatically in the moment is to make it a habit of always knowing what the current level of resources that a project has on hand as well as alternatives to the current course of action that could be undertaken if the situation were to change. While coming up with a list of possible scenarios to consider might seem daunting at first, the planning stage of any project is always bound to include offshoots that didn't pan out, they are a good place to start when it comes to alternatives.

The ability to look past the numbers: While a good project manager has the ability to act with almost robotic like precision when it comes to executing on a plan, that doesn't mean that they ignore the human component that comes along with it. The best project managers get to know each of their team members on a personal level and attune themselves to what is going on in their lives so that they can intervene as necessary. Not taking the time to understand the emotional state of the team can lead to serious consequences come crunch time and it will also make member of the team less likely to put the team ahead of their own personal goals and wellbeing and is therefore something that should be taken care of as soon as possible when a new team is created.

Chapter 3: Planning a Project Successfully

The first project you plan as a project manager can be extremely intimidating and with good reason, there are quite a lot of balls to keep in the area all at once and translating expectations into actions is always an intimidating prospect. To that end, you may find the following steps helpful when it comes to planning a successful project.

Put a face on the stakeholders: At the start of every project, it is important to take some time to consider who all the various stakeholders you are going to need to deal with in order to ensure the project proceeds successfully. The stakeholders for every project are going to be different and will always extend beyond just the people who hired you on as the project manager. Every stakeholder consideration will also need to include everyone who is going to be directly affected for the best results which includes users and potentially customers as well. Only by understanding just what stakeholders you are dealing with will you be able to generate a plan that adequately keeps all of their various interests in mind.

Once you have a clear idea of who all of your stakeholders are going to be you will then want to meet with all of them, or representatives from their groups, to frankly discuss their expectations as well as their needs and desires as a way of creating an outline when it comes to the scope of the project, its potential budget as well as a timeline for completion. The results from this exploratory exercise should ultimately manifest in what is known as a project scope statement. This document is considered the baseline document for the project and will include a detailed analysis of the scope of the project as well as the deliverables that will come into being at its completion.

It will also include the resources required to meet those deliverables in an effort to ensure that each of the key stakeholders and project generators is on the same page before any work has actually been completed. Your goal with this document is going to be digging deeper beyond simply fulfilling the shareholders stated desires and seeking out the root demand that is not being filled that is leading to them. Doing so will ensure that the benefits the project is projected to generate will really turn the heads of those you report too and help the project get off on the most productive foot possible.

Determine relevant goals as well as their overall importance: Once you have a scope statement that has been approved of, the next step will be to determine the various goals that the project will be striving to meet as well as their overall importance to shareholders based on the importance of the shareholders in question. Even the projects that are the most well supported at the start can easily run into a roadblock or two prior to completion, and it is important to know which goals you can most easily sacrifice first to ensure the completion of the project in some shape or form.

If you are having a hard time ranking your goals as they all seem either interconnected or equally important, you will find the best way to start is consider which goals are the most urgent and then work from there. While you will want to start by ranking your goals in order of importance, you will also need to take into account the stakeholder group that is served by each objective as well. It is sometimes going to be more important that every group is represented than it is to ensure the fourth or fifth most urgent goal get completed instead of the next, strictly speaking, down the line.

Consider Deliverables: With the goals that you are striving to hit clearly elucidated, the next thing you are going to want to do is determine exactly what it is your team is going to need to do to make each of the stated goals a reality, You are going to want to go into as much detail in this space as possible as you are going to need to have a very clear picture of every ounce of effort that will be required to make all of the goals a reality as well as who on the team is likely going to be doing the sweating. During this phase you are going to want to estimate due dates as well, though nothing will be finalized just yet. The goal in this step is to get a working estimate up and running, not to set a plethora of timetables in stone.

While it may be tempting to leave some prospective time tables blank, you will often find that once a time table is left open during the initial step of the process, it is more likely to be left open through the rest of the process as well. What's more, you will also typically find that tasks or goals without time tables are going to be the ones that are taken care of at the absolutely last moment possible every single time. Do yourself a favor and give your team clear deadlines in every step of the project, you will be glad you did in the long run.

When it comes to setting effective deadlines, it is important to give the team enough time to do the best job possible while at the same time not giving them enough time to slack around. A firm deadline is an excellent motivation tool, especially when you are dealing with individuals who are not especially committed to the project in question nor are they directly under your purview, leaving motivation difficult if not completely impossible otherwise. Additionally, having clear deadlines for every facet of the project will make it easier for you to track the progress of each, and in turn the progress of the project as a whole.

Finalize the schedule: With a general outline of the timeline in place for each individual goal that is part of the project, the next thing you are going to want to do is to research whatever is required to ensure that the timetables that you have created are going to be accurate throughout the length of the project. If you can do this type of research on your own then great, otherwise, it is perfectly acceptable to get your team in on the action assuming you can trust them to not pad out their estimates. If this is your first time working with a new group of individuals, then you are going to want to generate your own estimates in addition to listening to what they have to say in order to ensure that you can take them at their word in the future.

In addition to the timeframe for your new project, you are going to want to determine the amount of resources that is going to be required to see it through to completion as well as who among your team is best qualified to handle the assignment. Before making final assignments, however, it is important to put all of the tasks that you have outlined in order based on which need to be completed first. This is referred to as an order of dependency and it is the last piece of the puzzle you need to account for before you can put a firm plan into place.

When it comes to assigning team members to tasks it is important to remember that each team member is a finite resource which means that the best person for a given task might not always be the right person for the task at the moment. During this process it is important to start with the most important tasks as these are the ones that are going to have the least scheduling wiggle room. Once you have filled in these slots you can fill in the rest based on scheduling needs that will reveal themselves naturally.

Speculate about potential issues: With a general outline of the project coming together, the next thing you are going to want to consider are any potential issues that might arise based on all of the information that you have gathered so far. It is important to think about issues in a wider sense than just what could happen in the workplace, consider the time of the year and large local and national trends as well. Remember, the more potential issues you pinpoint early on, the more prepared you will be in case the worst actually does happen.

Present the plan: Once the plan is completed you will need to present it to the key stakeholders to ensure that they approve. That doesn't mean that the document you created has to match up with their expectations perfectly, however, though you will need to be ready to defend the changes if this is not the case. The plan you make should be an honest and realistic explanation of the plan in question, not a fairytale designed to get funding. Regardless of the results, the best plans are always those that are firmly based in reality.

Chapter 4: Keeping Stakeholders Happy

It doesn't matter what the size of the project you are overseeing is, every project has numerous different stakeholders of various importance and it is your job as  the project manager to ensure that they are all as relatively happy as can be expected. Unfortunately, this is going to be easier said than done as every type of stakeholder is naturally going to want something different regardless if it directly contradicts what another stakeholder requires at the same time. The job of the project manager then becomes about measuring happiness of various groups with the goal of keeping each as happy as possible while negatively affecting the others as little as possible at the same time. While this will certainly get easier with practice, if you are interested in something a little more tangible, consider the following.

Break down each goal: When it comes to keeping your stakeholders happy, the first thing you are going to want to do is break down each of your goals and determine how it relates to each of the different stakeholder groups you are working with. This way you will be able to track each grouping and report back to each interest group as progress is completed. Additionally, you are going to want to do your best to ensure that parts of the project that relate to each stakeholder group are worked on in tandem, when possible. This will automatically prevent accusations of favoritism from flying, regardless of how unfounded they actually are, and make your job much easier in the long run.

This process should be done early so that when scope is determined and requirements are drawn up, each of the relevant stakeholder groups is consider during this process as well. Again, sometimes it simply won't be feasible to pander to all of the relevant stakeholder groups at once as the steps in the process will forbid it. Even in these situations, however, you will always be glad you did the leg work and determined which goals align where, as the odds you will be asked about it at some point are quite high.

Determine stakeholder order: While it is nice to be able to make every group of stakeholders happy, the odds of this happening on a regular basis are much lower than you might prefer. To counteract this natural order of events, it is important to understand which stakeholders are naturally going to be more important than others. When it comes to determining order of importance, the first thing you are going to want to consider is the stakeholders that are funding the project. Regardless of what their ultimate role is, the project won't be completed if they are unhappy and pull the funding so as the project manager it is your job to ensure they are happy at the expense of everyone else if necessary.

The only exception to this rule is if one of your stakeholder groups is the customer and they are going to purchasing the end result of the project you are facilitating. If this is the case, then you can put the customer before the moneyed stakeholder you will want to ensure that you have the data to back up your claims. As a general rule, the moneyed stakeholder will primarily care about the bottom line which means that as long as what you are doing makes fiscal sense in the long run you can justify your actions.

Somewhere in the middle are the rest of the types of stakeholders, typically corporate employees who will often be utilizing the end result of the project as well. You will want to make an effort to prioritize their goals as they will often be utilizing the end result of the project the most, but unfortunately their needs are also the easiest to sacrifice when it comes to finding yourself with a shortened budget or timeline. Hope for the best with these types of goals but don't be afraid to use them as a way of preparing against the worst.

Determine the most important expectations: With the priority stakeholders identified, the next thing you will want to do is take a closer look at their specific goals of determining just what their expectations are going to be throughout the process. Your goal here is to determine at what points these expectations most accurately align with the objectives laid out for the project in question as well as the points where it noticeably adds value as well. The points when the two sets of data overlap are the expectations that you should put the most effort into seeing through to the fullest.

Early on you will likely find it difficult to determine which of a set of similar expectations will ultimately generate enough value for the business because you don't have the experience to tell how they both work out in the long run. When faced with something that you are unfamiliar with, you will generally find the best course of action to be to perform a risk analysis on each and then act on the one with the lower overall amount of risk. Just because a prominent stakeholder's request seems sound at first blush, doesn't mean it is actually worth prioritizing, risk analysis will save you time and money in the long run.

Project promotion: The project manager is the person in charge of communicating with all the various pieces of the project to keep all the balls in the air for as long as possible. A natural part of that communication then is going to be talking up the project in one way or another to all of the stakeholders who might need a morale boost at some point between when the project starts and when it raps up successfully. While short projects aren't going to require a concentrated marketing effort, those that are longer or are likely going to need a second influx of capital will need to be treated like any other product and marketed aggressively at their target audience.

In this case, marketing the project successfully means taking the research you have already done on all of the various stakeholders and spinning things so that it sounds like the goals that they have for the project in question are almost ready to be presented (and they really are quite swell) if only you had a little more time. In addition to spreading the word to stakeholders directly, you will also want to work to pass along the message in a grassroots fashion. While certain stakeholders might not be swayed by what you have to say directly, if the same information were to instead make it back to them through the grapevine then that might be a different situation entirely. The key to success is to know your stakeholders, know what they are interested in and never lie about anything. Presenting facts in a positive fashion is one thing, outright lying is another and will always prove to be the wrong choice in the long run.

Ensure that the lines of communication are always open: While initially it is perfectly natural for you to be the one reaching out to all of the various types of stakeholders that you have to deal with. Over time you are going to want to foster a relationship that ensures information instead flows both ways. The goal in this instance is to make each stakeholder or stakeholder representative feel as though you are genuinely looking out for their best efforts and that you goal is to help them as much as possible. If stakeholders feel as though it is in their best interests, they will contact you directly about fears or concerns that you might have which, in turn, makes it much easier for you to quell those fears as quickly and permanently as possible.

What's more, if they feel as though they have your ear when it comes to suggestions or additions to the project, regardless of if they make it into the final results or not they will feel more committed to the project in question. This type of buy-in can often be crucial to the long term success of difficult projects and it is recommended that you cultivate it as early on as possible.

Manage expectations: Finally, throughout every step of the process you should be subtly balancing out the expectations various stakeholders have for the project with the reality of the direction things are currently heading. It is amazing how much more agreeable various stakeholders can be to the fact that their goals have been cut due to costs if they are slowly lead to the fact that it is happening over time instead of finding out about it all at once. Remember, it is important to still always spin things in a positive light, while at the same time being realistic about the results that should be expected, the only one at fault if stakeholders are disappointed when all is said and done is you.

Chapter 5: Communicating Effectively

When a project is going well it can be easy to put off communicating regularly until things start to turn and if things are currently difficult it can be easy to wait until things  settle down to start regular communication. While the differences behind these two approaches are significant, their end result is the same and your overall successful project completion rate is sure to suffer if you follow either of them regularly. Follow the tips below for communicating as effectively throughout a project as possible in order to improve your overall success rate every single time.

Create a communication plan

When it comes to ensuring that every relevant player in a given project is communicated with properly, many project managers find that it is helpful to start off the project with a complete communication plan to go along with the other plans that they have created. An effective communication plan ensures that no one is ever going to be left out of the loop once the project really gets up and running by taking into account all of the issues the project is going to face and planning out beforehand how to ensure communication will remain regular regardless.

Start with the basics: When it comes time to create your own communication plan you are going to want to start by taking into account the various types of communication that are going to be required of you throughout the process. This not only means face to face, over the phone and text based communications but things like meetings or presentations as well. Regularly scheduled meetings are the backbone of a clearly communicated project as it easily allows all interested parties to remain on the same page quickly and effectively. From there it is just a matter of determining who will need to be invited to what meetings and how often their presence will be requested.

Standardize a plan: When it comes to deciding just what types of information will need to be communicated between yourself and various stakeholders or team members it is best to adopt a standardized plan for group communication before varying it based on the individuals present at the meeting in question. By making an effort to ensure as much of your information is uniform as possible, you minimize the possibility of providing different groups with different takes on the same information, in turn minimizing the number of issues you have to deal with in the long run at the same time. Remember, small variances in the data provided can lead to major differences in the long term which is why it is important to standardize this information as much as you possibly can every time you have the opportunity to do so.

Remember, the key to effective communication is providing the proper information at the proper time to the correct audience, thus ensuring that they take the presented information and use it in the way you want them to. This means that while you will want to ensure the baseline information remains the same, the way you frame and present it to each different portion of your team is extremely important to the overall success of the project as well. You will want to have an idea of the types of communication you will need to have with each group and update them at regular intervals throughout the life of the project.

Choose a tool for the task

Use a Power/Interest Grid: A power interest grid is a useful way of determining how in the loop you need to keep various stakeholders throughout the life of any given project. To utilize this tool, you are going to want to create a simple grid that is split into four sections based on the amount of power a stakeholder has and how interested they are in the project in question. If a stakeholder has little power over the project as well as little interest in it then you will want to monitor them for any change but otherwise you can safely them alone without worry. If, on the other hand, they have little actual power but are interested in what is going on then there is no harm in keeping them informed of major milestones in the project as they are met and surpassed. If the stakeholder is powerful and disinterested, then all you need to worry about is keeping them satisfied without getting into the nitty gritty that they will likely have no use for. Finally, if a stakeholder is both powerful and interested then you are going to need to keep a very close watch on them to ensure things proceed smoothly.

While not a useful tool when it comes to dealing with the specific behavior of individual stakeholders, the power/interest grid can be a useful tool for basing your initial plans on, as long as you make a point of updating it with additional information once it becomes available and you have a clearer idea of just what each stakeholder is going to require from you specifically. It is important to always strive to update the initial analysis of various stakeholders once the plan for the project has been accepted and again once it reaches the midway point towards its completion to ensure that it continues to be an effective judge of the current situation.

Ishikawa Diagram: When it comes to deciding what potential issues relating to the project in question need to be shared with which members of the team along with the relevant stakeholders, a good place to start is with an Ishikawa diagram which is commonly called a fish bone diagram as well. To utilize this tool effectively, you will need to determine the primary problem that is being addressed before then breaking it down into relevant categories, one category for each stakeholder as well as one for the project team. Problems that are a subset of the overall problem that needs to be solved are then listed off of each of the categories in order of relevance. While it seems simple, it is an easy way to organize all of the problems that a project is facing while clearly delineating which group of team members needs to deal with what in order to remain effective and see the project through to completion in the given timeline with the expected resources.

Create a responsibility assignment matrix: A responsibility assignment matrix, commonly known as a RACI matrix is a great way to promote effective communication between team members. RACI is an acronym that is short for Responsible, Accountable, Consulted, Informed. A RACI chart includes a number of columns with different information based tasks as well as several rows relating to each task that needs to be completed during the life of the project. You will then assign a specific team member to each task and make it clear to the rest of the team who they can speak with if they have questions about the relevant type of information. If there is a constant stream of new information coming at your team on a regular basis, this is a great way to get it out there without taking up everyone's time in doing so.

Be careful not to give out too much information: As a project manager, it is entirely likely that you are going to constantly be receiving a steady stream of information that is tangentially related to several parts of the project or tasks that are currently being performed. While technically you might have a slim reason to share that information with the section of the team working on that project, doing so would distract them from whatever it is they are currently working on, thus negatively affecting the project as a whole. As such, it is your job to provide information when asked, but to otherwise withhold irrelevant information and hold back on relevant information until it is required or until otherwise scheduled periods of communication to ensure that the workflow remains as smooth and constant as possible.

To this end it is important to be aware of the cadence of the information that you provide as well as the content that is being shared. Even if it is just in email form, you will be surprised at how much time during the day can be wasted from a handful of unnecessary emails. Even if each email takes only a single minute out of a team member's day, if there are 10 people on your team and you send twelve separate emails instead of one well thought out and clear email then you are already out two hours from the day without actually accomplishing much of anything. Finally, when communicating digitally it is important to consider the relationship you have with the reader and do what you can to drive that relationship home to ensure the best results.

Chapter 6: Seeing it Through to Completion

While lots of planning will certainly never hurt, seeing a project through to completion will always involve dealing with plenty of unforeseen issues effectively in order to  get the job done. Consider the following suggestions and remember that what separates the best project managers from the rest is their dedication, determination and the results that they produce time and again.

Dealing with roadblocks

The first thing you are going to want to keep in mind when it comes to dealing with roadblocks is that the best way to get started is to take a step back from the situation in question in an effort to provide yourself with a bit of perspective. While it is only natural to want for every task to be finished precisely on time, it is rarely going to be a matter that leads to either ultimate success or failure for the project in question. While a single roadblock can easily create a chain reaction of issues it is important to look at what has happened rationally and take the time that would traditionally be spend denying the issue and wishing it had never happened and instead spend that time trying to mitigate the results as completely as possible.

Remember, once an issue has occurred every minute that you let it go unchecked is a minute that you let it get worse instead of mitigating its impact. This means you are going to want to compare the current situation with your initial plan before then determining all the different ways that you can go about ensuring the project remains on track. When making a list it is important to give yourself time to think clearly, if you made a list of possible issues as suggested then you are already going to be streets ahead when it comes to solving your problem, but even if you haven't you will not want to rush as rushed solutions are often poor solutions.

With a variety of solutions at hand all you will need to do is to determine which goals you have that can be sacrificed successfully as a way of getting around the roadblock and what that will mean for the project as a whole. Once you have mapped various goals to various solutions you should easily be able to determine which is of the least importance and then work to implement the plan accordingly.

When working through the process outlined above, you will also want to go out of your way to ensure that your team remains as calm and focused on the end result as possible. As the project manager your goal is to minimize issues that can affect the project as thoroughly as you can, and this means ensuring that everyone around you keeps a cool head and, more team loses their cool after an announcement you only have yourself to blame.

Resolving conflicts
Even if the project that you are working on doesn't involve different departments or numerous different points of view all contributing to the common good you are still likely to run into personality conflicts between individuals for any one of a countless number of reasons. As the project manager it is important that you take it upon yourself to resolve these conflicts as quickly and positively as possible to ensure that they don't negatively impact the timeline for project completion any more than they have already.

As the team leader, you may or may not already have existing ties to certain members of the team more than others; while this is perfectly normal, especially in smaller companies, it is important that you are aware of these connections so that you can make it clear that they do not have anything to do with the conflict resolution results that are ultimately decided upon. Depending on the severity of the relationship in question, bringing in an outside mediator might be the best choice, anything that can be done to ensure it appears as though you acted impartially is always going to be the right choice.

When faced with this type of scenario you are going to want to try and find out as much about the incident in question before speaking with those involved separately at first in an effort to piece together the whole story. You will then typically want to bring both individuals together and have each of them present their side of the story so that all parties can be aware of all sides of the issue. If the mutual understanding that this provides does not seem to be effective, the next thing you will want to do is take control of the interaction by laying out the heart of the matter as you see it before asking the arguing parties how they would then proceed. As a general rule, if you can get all the involved parties to agree on a solution you will find better results overall.

If the conflict in question is ultimately going to come down to an either or scenario, then it is going to be your job as the project manager to be the ultimate arbiter of a verdict. If this responsibility falls to you, it is important to not falter in the delivery of your verdict as in so doing you weaken your perceived authority greatly in the eyes of your team. If you are unsure of who is right and who is wrong all you can do is spend as much time researching the issue as possible before ultimately casting your vote and sticking with it. Again, it doesn't matter who you side with, it only matters that you do so with authority and then stick with the decision that has been made.

The only exception to this is rule is when new evidence is presented at a later date that makes the previous decision obviously incorrect. You want to be seen as a decisive leader, not one that refuses to admit when they are wrong. Stick to your guns, but only when it is the right thing to do.

Conclusion

Thank for making it through to the end of *Project Management: A Practical Beginners Guide to Becoming a Master Project Manager with Any Project*, let's hope it was informative and able to provide you with all of the tools you need to achieve your goals whatever it is that they may be. Just because you've finished this book doesn't mean there is nothing left to learn on the topic expanding your horizons is the only way to find the mastery you seek.

The next step is to stop reading already and to get ready to manage your first project as effectively as possible. By this point it is only natural that you are ready to stop preparing and start acting on the things that you have learned, but in so doing you are only going to be opening yourself up to a greater chance at failure. Successfully managing a project is as much about planning out how the project should go as it is about ensuring that the various cogs in the wheel of the project all move as smoothly as possible. As such, only by focusing equally on both parts of the equation will you be able to find the true success that you seek. While the road ahead might seem difficult and full of roadblocks, success is possible if you commit to the task at hand fully and promise yourself to never give up. Becoming a great project manager is a marathon, not a sprint, slow and steady wins the race.

Finally, if you found this book useful in anyway, a review on Amazon is always appreciated!